Interim
Nation

Alan M. Kent

Interim Nation

Poems

First published by Francis Boutle Publishers
272 Alexandra Park Road
London N22 7BG
Tel/Fax: 020 8889 7744
Email: info@francisboutle.co.uk
www.francisboutle.co.uk

ISBN 978 0 9935344 0 9

Acknowledgements

I would like to thank the editors of the magazines and publications which first published many of the poems here. These include *An Baner Kernewek, Bardhonyeth Kernow, Brittle Star, The Clearing, Cornish Story, Earth Love, Murder of Krows 2, The Rialto* and *Rubies in the Darkness*. Several of the poems were originally published in *Wave Hub: New Poetry of Cornwall* and have featured on BBC Radio Cornwall and BBC Radio 4. 'Cornish Shovel' and 'Ode on the Mylor Hoard' won the English verse category of the Cornish Gorsedd Poetry competitions in 2010 and 2012 respectively. 'Cornishman's Dam, Gabriel's Gully, Otago, New Zealand' was runner-up in the 2013 English verse competition of the Cornish Gorsedd. 'The Road to Brega' was a runner up in the 2012 Torbay Poetry Competition.

Alan M Kent, 2015

Probus / Lanbrebois
Truro / Truru
Cornwall / Kernow

Contents

Poems

I

Mermaid's Purse

From this distance,
       on the tide-line,
       you could be a black, horned beetle;
       your membrane shimmering with salt,
and ready to snap those jagged jaws tight shut.

This, or a tiny fruit bat taking rest,
       woven in leather and bladderwrack,
       you are a minute Gothic structure.
       Strewn on expanse of strand,
you've evolved as if to creep and float at once.

Closer, and I know you
       as the clasp of the Mermaid,
       as much a part of her,
       as mirror and comb, scale and tail.
You glisten the way she did, to poor Mathey Trewella.

Black, brown, olive and yellow,
       you carry a beard of seaweed,
       or maybe even ringlets of your hair,
       gone wild and wanton in current and tides.
Now you are adrift on white sand and grey pebble.

All of this is lore though,
       carved into bench ends,
       told by men to make the world magical,
       the way humans do with everything
they do not understand, or wish not to know.

Yet you know your own poetry purse.
       You are egg capsule,
       fragile case of collagen,
       your hatchling already gone,
floating now with real beasts of the deep.

Tendrils clasp at air and nothing,
      showing that your rays are bred.
      Proteins decompose; myths deconstruct.
      Soon, on the high tide
you will be pulled back to your watery world.

Now in the dryness of my hand
      my fingers feel your knots and swirls.
      The purse carries no coins, no plunder.
      Instead, in its small nation
is broad continuity of life; embryo of us all.

The Ecology of Language Evolution, Launceston, Tasmania

My people have a rare beauty
   – the non-standard way they speak.
   It is not visible.
         It is temporal,
      but grows natural as rainforest.

It might not last long
   – and go the way of that other fractured tongue of ours.
   Let's not let it go,
        Let it not go
      the way of the Tasmanian tiger.

Open your jaw 120 degrees
   – just like the Thyalcine - and yell:
   Extinction is not an option here.
        Instead, preserve.
   Fight for sustainability.

That beauty can travel thousands of miles
   – I've heard it loud and clear.
   The way the people here say Lan'son
        keeps the species in tact.
      Language succeeds, where marsupial did not.

I do not want sightings
   – shadows, glimpses, footprints.
   Instead, sustain ut.
        Speak un proud. Speak un broad.
   Let me always hear the soul of ee.

Devices

Best show it off,
or else others will think
they're a loser,
without friends,
without connectivity,
without somebody needing them.

There is an infinite variety
of headphones,
wires,
adaptors,
plug-ins,
and screens,
Some work two at once:
double the need to be in touch.
What won't wait
that used to be unsaid or unspoken?
Does the instant fashion all?

One day, us humans will evolve
with palms already embedded
with Samsung, Sony or Apple.
I see a thousand Hornby train sets
where perfect plastic people
stand on station platforms
gazing at tiny screens,
and missing the 125
to Paddington.

Instead, I read, think
and watch the earth turn.
I try to say what is needed,
not what is not.

How nice
not to have a device.

Agony

Longing hurts the most.

The want.
The need.
The craving

       to hold you

   bites.

It consumes,
floors me,
takes me away
from poetry, history, hope.

Instead, there is just longing.

To be human is this.

If I had known
I'd have bothered
with nothing else.

For you, I would have
      always reached.

      Always migrated.

      Always.

The Gift of a Sea Urchin

You ask for something
that costs little,
but represents me – *is* me.

I give you a sea urchin,
stacked near an honesty box,
with 50p for the RNLI.

Its sharp spines have gone
but the crenulation's still rough.
Its hard pink and brown pleases.

I'm not sure what you'll make of it.
You're sad maybe,
that this is just a shell.

But it smells of the ocean,
it was built in the waves and sand
near me – just like me .

There is a basket of them
at Charlestown,
but I've selected just one.

I see your hand
feel its symmetry,
scoop around the petaled mouth.

They fracture easily these things.
One slip and it'll shatter:
shell quickly becoming shore.

Years ago, the nick-nack shops
of bustling Mevagissey
made them into lamps.

That is not its fate here.
Instead, I hope its globe
will become your world.

Here, take it please.
Now you know I am this, and this is me
never wondering, never searching.

A Normalisation of Relations

was there ever a moment
       of true unity?
did completeness
       ever pass your way?

i am coming to think
       this far in this day,
this hour, this minute,
       that there was not.

we are all too awkward,
       too complex,
too twisted
       to ever converge.

we sit close then,
but never close enough.
we try but we are flawed
       and human.

we are though,
       ever-hopeful, until the last,
yet normality seeps in,
       and helps us come to terms with love.

Costos Papiano

who should have been a Greek legend,
was found dead in his chair at fifty.
Been there for days apparently,
rotting like frail pages of the *Iliad*.
He was never destined for greatness,
with his full beard at thirteen,
his shuffling, unconfident gait
and green parka, down to his knees.

He was always destined to be a victim,
unending prey for bullies;
a life sat before endless CSI dvds,
his weekly outing to ASDA,
the knowing he never really did fit
and that whatever alternative life
had been planned by the Gods
hadn't showed up yet.

His was now all dole, day care,
and a maisonette back Nanpean.
I doubt he ever knew love,
except the stoked breath of his ma
dropping her fag ash inta' the pasties
and in the steady side-crimping
regretting the day she ever had her eye turned
by Pap's feythur, who had hair like Elvis.

It is 1975 Pap, and you and I
are playing *Six Million Dollar Man*
high on the heathered Acropolis of Beacon Hill,
pushing through slow-mo sand and mica.
Then, ethnicity or history had no say.
We wuz Bionic; made of metal and wire.
Always: 'Gentlemen, we can rebuild him'
What Steve Austin faced, then we too.

Beacon Hill still watches
and since then I have read *Iliad* and more.
I know how men become legend.
The day I hear of his death,
the tv that once brought back Austin from the dead
reminds me that Pap has become clay.
There comes news from a continent away
that downtrodden Greece has had its say.

Bucket List

Daily, I am sent
'100 Places you MUST SEE before you die.'
Today, a day when I am still alive,
I scan through the chosen exotica.

I have not seen the Pyramids of Giza.
I have not climbed into mist at Machu Picchu.
I have not felt the carvings on the temple at Angkor Wat.

Neither have I been to Red Square,
or walked the Great Wall of China,
or stood in front of the Taj Mahal.
I have missed meets and greets on the Maldives.

They are places that must wait.
I for them, and them for me.
Some will wait an eternity.

I am grateful though, for the few I have made,
I have walked beneath the trilithons at Stonehenge.
I have climbed to the top of the Sears Tower,
I have driven across the Golden Gate Bridge.

I am grateful too,
for all those places and people on my bucket list
who I have witnessed or have kissed.

Older I wax,
yet waxing lyrical over what I MUST SEE
only comes to repel me.

Instead, I take pleasure in the ordinary.
The poet writes about
what others don't want me to SEE.

So, I have seen food banks on my street,
I have seen human rights abused,
I have seen the earth being killed.

Nothing fancy I know,
but just the clanking pail
at which the poet always wanted to give a kick.
I'll ignore wish lists and MUST SEEs.
My Facebook page I will freeze.

Now before you go – and pass on,
write your bucket list.
Think of what really counts:
loved ones, lovers, family, friends:
the ones who'll remember you
when kicked buckets call,
and you meet and greet your exotic end.

Kepler 438b

You are, we are told,
the most likely planet
to support life.

You are an 'alien' earth,
potential ark,
13% larger than we are.

You have all the conditions for life.
You lie in the habitable zone.
Maybe you do exist.

From here,
you seem joyous,
just like our earth.

No wars.
No disagreements.
No boundaries.

And I wonder if you are
treated the same
as we treat earth?

Are your seas polluted?
Do your icecaps melt?
Do you kill all that you should love?

Then I wonder:
how do you treat your people?
The same capitalism, lies and terror.

Are there, in your wonder,
any people like us –
small people?

– where rights go unchallenged,
history goes unchecked,
where recognition seems... well... still a universe away...

To be sure, even on such a paradise,
it sounds impossible,
and we know the truth.

Time and distance
always re-write history
and who gets to hold the pen.

No doubt it's the same on 438b.
Some lie prostrate on the floor,
while others stride onwards above.

Best make sure
we never truly find you
Earth, Version 2.0.

Where have you gone Gus Honeybun?

Where have you gone Gus Honeybun?
We need you now.

We need you Gus
in these dark days of IEDs,
high petrol prices
and the loneliness of *Facebook*.

We nee you Augustus J
in these tense times of iPads,
the war on terror
and Saturday night Blue-Ray.

You were there for me once,
when that July, I turned six,
and you gave me six bunny hops.
To think – my name on the TV,

I was made up.
It made my world complete,
in a time before You Tube,
web cams and texting.

I watched transfixed
at your slot, puppet rabbit,
with your winks, head-stands
and way you could 'turn out the lights'.

We need you Gus,
with your wide-eyed innocence
to tell us it will be alright,
to give us birthdays all over again.

We need you to just be the preview
to jelly and ice-cream,
pass the parcel
and all those hopeful wishes.

Where have you gone Gus Honeybun?
We need you now more than ever.

It seems you have gone,
like all the other magic
that defined we peninsula kids,
we naïve rabbit-loving viewers.

You have gone the way of the piskies,
gone the way of mermaids,
gone the way of knockies,
and gone the way of me.

I'm here writing to you Gus
– *Love from Uncle Al and the dog* –
Just the way Ian Stirling
read out the card on air.

Wherever you are Gus,
I want an ear waggle
and please,
press the magic button.

Watching *Origo Mundi*, Cubitt Park, London

for Guy Watson

There you are God.
　　　　I never imagined you that way.

Adam. And Eve.
　　　　How long have your lines been unspoken?

Cain and Abel played as blood brothers,
　　　　united, then thin as water.

Of course that's how Noah was done.
　　　　And yes, ark and animals are one.

See the walls of the Red Sea part,
　　　　This Moses is Everyman.

I watch Solomon's temple grow
　　　　in a revamped King's Cross.

I've known you for so long
　　　　and now to see you live

is oil of mercy,
　　　　true rood indeed.

Now you may
　　　　plant an apple pip upon my tongue.

Cuckoo Feast

Towednack Church is a granite tor
      the devil forgot to round off.
It stands square to ocean and moor,
      accepting anything this nation throws at it.

On a bugger of a day like today
      you may swim up the aisles,
take a lugger to the altar,
      tie un off afore the pulpit's pier.

This far west, this far into Atlantic's dread
      every parish has a legend.
They were there before
      each priest and you party stepped on in.

Here at the home of Tewennocus,
      legend comes as a tree stump
thrown on a fire in late winter,
      and out of which flew a cuckoo.

The farmers had gathered only
      to sit warm against moorland chill,
but instead, somehow raised the dead
      and made a phoenix through inaction.

The secretive bird was symbol of life,
      of summer come again,
of the mysterious cycles of life and death
      that only Tewennocus knew.

To commemorate they set a fiddler forth,
      who'd play this time, each year.
Up on the towers and spires of the hills
      cuckoos turn to hear the strain.

The phoenix nation surrounding the church
       unfolds like a perfect picture book
and the western sky deceives all.
          The cuckoo calls Avast – and all becomes still.

The Smell of Cornish Methodism

It is there still.

You travel thousands miles
but it remains,
locked deep
in the corners of Gunwen,
in the Sunday School of Trethosa,
in the air of Rescorla.

The mix is of dusty plaster,
a white bubbling in the walls,
giving off the lime and cement of the pre-modern,
trace elements of hymnals,
once pristine published once by Netherton and Worth,
the surprise of Anniversary prizes:
the glue of labels stuck in the front pages of a Joseph Hocking novel.
Ink and calligraphy not seen any more.

There too, is that wonderful dampness
that follows my people around the globe:
mould, moss, rain, and rot –
the richness of decay and disintegration.
Pure entropy.
This tells me the way things must be.
This shows me, reminds me, of our will and purpose.

There is the trace of furniture polish,
the harsh bleach in the toilets,
the nuggets of green soap.
Cleanliness is next to Godliness.
All of this chimes in.

In cups lurks the smell of 10,000 cups of taa,
hundreds of packets of custard creams,
the great trays of Anniversary buns
saffron as big as your head,
tea-treats, sweat and snail-creeps on hot July afternoons.

Here too is the odour
of boys with collar and tie,
dressed up from claywork for Sunday,
pressed pink into tight shirt,
and laced with Old Spice.

Old nudges of perfume still sit in the aisles,
from the women who changed the flewers each week,
and wiped the crockery clean,
yanked out from the Belfast sinks.

Sometimes, there lingers
the smell of the fear of damnation,
the frightened farts of those guilty
or those who had sinned.
All is tempered by dust and the smell of time,
the knowing that this never changes.

Sometime this is more than chapel tough.
Sometimes, this is the smell of my flawed nation itself,
each chapel a microcosm of this land
of pulpit and organ, of pump and pares.

And yet in travels too,
the same smells have I encounteerd,
in Grass Valley, Colorado,
in the iron chapels of Mineral Point,
the slate of Pennsylvania,
it is there – poking at me,
reminding me of home,
of the strands of my DNA.
It is there wherever my people
choose to erect a chapel.

It is familiar as cooking on a range,
fresh pasties,
splits of thunder and lightning.

One day, I shall die in it
and my soul, like all those others before me,
shall merge and flow.

In this
I shall become Wesley's breath,
and all shall be well.

The Road to Brega

'I neither love nor yet am free,
  For though the flame I find
Be not intense in the degree
  'Tis of the purest kind.'
'Fair Friend, 'Tis True Your Beauties Move' by Sidney Godolphin
(1610-1643)

Yet it sounds so resolutely Cornish, that place
on the Gulf of Sirte, in the sultry Ajdabliya district,
the most southerly point of the Mediterranean's reach,
where ancient Europe ends and modern Africa begins.
It is not the Brythonic Bre ['Hill' in my halting Troyance tongue].
Instead, it is beautiful Arabic: مرسى البريقة [*Marsa el-Brega*].

Read it aloud. It is a scrawl as magical, as holy, as pure
as all those lost manuscripts of sinners and saints at Restormel
that went up in bitter Parliamentarian flames.
Maybe, there is some cloaked Indo-European connection,
linguistic lineage scat over miles and millennia
that binds both sand and sea, the Arab and the Celt.

This deserted Brega though, still sounds like
where I d'live, graw, eat, sleep, write an' love.
Here – and there – every place-name has its own poetry.
The Libyan opposition march onwards, over it.
just like our blacksmith Michael Joseph, our tough Thomas Flamank
who once stanked another long road to freedom.

Men there be on the rawd t'Brega see,
spoken as if they must al'ays be afore pilcher or camel.
Cummis-zon you. We got a revolution t'win boy.
They d'knaw that soon, they could be daid as a 'ammer,
lost t' Muammar Gaddafi's grizzled forces
– an' ee who don't knaw nuff t'knaw ee dun't knaw nothun.'

At these Live-in-the-Sirte-Oil-field SKY news reports
and UN-sanctioned Tornado bombing missions

I cannot help but think of other uncivil chaos, other civil wars:
the way once these bickering islands walked long roads
to Stamford Hill, Lostwithiel and Lansdowne
and felt too, the taste of their divided land rupturing black.

This was how boy Godolphin, proud courtier and poet
signed up fur freedom in the *Lismore Papers*
an' comed t'be shot in a skirmish at Chagford in Devon.
Es, the tiring road *t'Marsa el*-Chagford, 1643...
Ee died slowly in the porch of the Three Crowns Hotel.
Another warrior poet gone on see, fightun' fur the truth.

The long road t'Brega is a brave bit baissly,
lined with burnt-out Mercedes trucks, craters and body bags.
The convoy air is now sick with death's stench, but still they walk.
Godolphin knew this as he climbed the black *bre* of Dartmoor
and walked steadfast by the side of stylish Sir Ralph Hopton.
In his mind, the unfinished words of 'The Passion of Dido for Æneas'

West of this present-day carnage, in Carthage, pure as snow,
she did all she could for him: for hope, for love, for passion.
In burning Brega, they do the same, this bright April day.
Seventy men train with seven rifles, while dated artillery jams.
Men who can hardly stand join boys who don't yet shave.
It is always the way: all Godolphins have their day on the hill.

So in Western Libya, the liberating army is more rag-tag,
Nike t-shirts and Liverpool tops blend with AK-47s.
Call of Duty: Black Ops on the PS3 is now all too real.
For BBC camera crews, injuries and bandages are badges of honour.
A new passion will be written on the blasted tank armour:
If regimes in Tunisia and Egypt can topple, then why not here?

Don't you see it? Are you that unsure still?
This an old, proud country; an old, proud people
– just as old as those crotchety, yet childish West Britons
who cling onto the towering cliffs of a salty, slatey, sour-tasting land

that seemingly gave them up for dead centuries ago.
And yet, still, Brega, Carn Brea, Breannick…

We. They. We. Still on that road. That long road.
It feels like countries come and go so quickly now.
They rid themselves of tyranny, hostile regimes
despots, dictators, oppressors, Macbeths of the mind
who have their vaulting ambition snapped and shorn.
Then, and only then, may the flames of hope flicker into life.

We know not our land still: anathemas like 'County' still hurt.
Freedom is curtailed on Carn Brea, at Breannick's Atlantic swash.
On to Brega then: مرسى البريقة [*Marsa el-Brega*].
Sometimes civil wars never end: they are infinite.
At least on our long, slow road to revolution,
we have the lasting consolation of good Godolphin's purest love.

Nebra Sky Disc

Hard to see
> any religious significance,
> or even judge it
> as an astronomical instrument.

Standing here at Nebra,
> in Saxony-Anhalt,
> you sit more like a child's toy:
> a blue and gold shield,
> dented by a wooden sword's sturdy hits.

Most obviously,
> you are a face:
> one eye wide open;
> the other winking,
> above a smiley mouth,
> like some drug-fuelled memory of Acid House.

You could be
> the colour of the sea at Porthcurno,
> your bronze the dredges of the ocean,
> left at Pedn Vounder at low tide.
> Your crescent moon is the Logan rocking.

I like this object's edges:
> the feel of elephant's feet,
> or even the crimped edge of a pasty,
> where metal is tucked behind metal,
> for decoration and whimsy.

You are small:
> 30cm in diameter,
> but what you depict is vast.
> You tell a story told nowhere else
> in ancient art.

These are the heavens:
        sun and moon, a lunar crescent,
        and the Pleiades
        nestled into a blue-green patina.

Someone
        understood that we revolve around the sun –
        and had you made 1600 years
        before the birth of Christ.

                Old magic then.

In trekking to Germany though,
        I do nothing special.
        Its mystery would be enough
        and yet, we know a little more.

                The gold that shimmers
                was direct from Helston's River Cober.
                They are pieces of *hal-an-tow*.

                This tin too,
                from my interim nation.
                They are Stannary and spall.

I grasp at the journeys:
        the distances, the providences,
        and slowly,
        blindly,
        the now.

                Who were the hands that picked up the nuggets?

                Who traded ingots at Ictis?

These questions bite
       the same way
       the heavens intrigued its maker.

Such knowledge
       must have made him feel incomplete:
       Knowing only a little,
       and wanting more.

Now, as I view this disk,
       at an exhibtion:
       Der geschmiedete Himmel,
such knowledge of the 'smithied sky'

       can make my land complete.

Montol

This is Olivia's "allowed foolery".
It is the world gone topsy-turvy.
But these are no brigands.
Instead, they are the joyous celebrants.

Inversion is the order of the night
with bishops and mock mayors
shown as the dullards they are.
For perverse ridicule, they are set.

The people trundle through the streets
hauling a great box of light:
a coffin of hope, a lozenge of life,
at this bleakest point in the year.

It is carnival of resistance,
renewal and resurgence,
no longer at the mercy
of prissy clerks and frowning Methodists.

Like in much of our half-baked state,
the Pagan and Christian fuse
into spirit of the soul,
into vital bond and acceptance.

All can be as they ought.
All can be as they want.
This is Crowley and Christ,
both Grimore and Bible black.

Masks and disorder reign
in this festival of winter
Thread your way down Chapel Sreet,
and into Davy's Market Jew.

Musicians and dancers
flock in black and feathers,

and, by drum and fiddle
coax the new year on.

Mock the upper classes
with top hats and tails.
Sing and tumble in a slice
of pre-modern guise.

It is over in a night
but each year, we are fortunate
that such foolery, such balance
calls back the light from the black.

II

Purgations

Uncle had a way of dealing
with the buggers.

"Boil up Kiddle!" he'd shout
to missus inside.

And the Morphy Richards
went into steamy overdrive.

I'd follow – as apprentice inquisitor,
as he tipped in the boiling water

though the cracks in the concrete
and into the ant's nest.

The tsunami hit instantly,
wrecking intricately-crafted caverns

sluicing through tunnels,
destroying, in one wave, the whole colony.

A civilisation could be smashed
on one hot July afternoon.

I was fascinated by the agony.
intrigued how this micro-world would cope.

The cruelty of it was addictive.,
and even ennobling somehow.

Years later, knowing the adult I am,
I reflect on the massacre

I realise the power,
realise something innate:

the way we like to eradicate,
the way we stop nations

getting above themselves,
becoming too grand.

Expectations

First, the hologram security checks;
then, the turning of endless locks.
Cages open inwards
and purposefully creak.
I am given an escort,
as we head into the belly
of this Napoleonic beast.
All smells of detergent.
Thick, paint-coated radiators throb.
There is a yelling somewhere.
Stark courtyards are planted-up now
but they still have a grey authority.
You can't disguise it: the menace.
My mind moves inescapably
to slop buckets,
broad arrows.
and *Porridge.*

Out there, beyond the barbed wire, is Whiteworks:
marshland and quagmires
by the old tin-streaming pits
a wilderness of space and freedom
where, still as a naive boy
I camped and walked
and learnt the words and lore of this moor:
Crockern, Wistman's Wood,
Uncle Tom Cobley and all.

Now, work brings me to this HMP
as tutor for my egalitarian University.
I am at once reformer, educator, and believer.
Many are not.

The education block is underfunded –
an Eliot Hut of hardboard walls,
class-rooms of chalk-dust and damp.
(no white boards here)

There are yards of books never opened.

I know 8 out of 10 prisoners have poor literacy.

My client enters
in a confusion of hand-shakes –
or was it me not wishing to really touch the reality of crime?

He's a lifer. His letter told me that.
He is my age. He could be me.

Today, of all things, our text is *Great Expectations*.
He has already been marched through
Fathers and Sons, *Pride and Prejudice*. the plays of Aphra Behn.
So Chapter One then:
Hulks, Magwitch, a file and a pork pie.
The irony is almost too much for me.
I can barely read Dickens' prose.

Outside, a light snow is falling
on those tors I once walked,
peering down on this prison hulk
set in the Princetown ocean.
As my lifer reads Abel Magwitch's words
– "And you know what wittles is?" –
I am left speechless,
dumb-founded,
silent as sleet.

Weeks later, his scrawled assignment arrives by post.
It is handwritten and there's a note with it –
'No computers in here.'
As I read his reasoned words,
I think of all the shackles
opened, pulled against, shaken
for him to get here.

I see him at work in his cell,
breaks between chapters.
to look out over those same tors;
the endeavour to educate self, understand
to go beyond experience so far.
I read his delight that Abel's a gentleman at heart:
a hidden benefactor no less.
It is lore a lifer likes.

The envelope this work arrives in
is marked 'Crown Property'.
What lies within is owned
by none, but him.
Imagining out to river, moor, tor,
there is, at least,
a moment's freedom
shackled to his words.
The essay makes him someone else.

Suddenly, I am Pip looking back.
And from the marshes,
for my escaping convict,
some sustaining wittles I have brought.

Occupations

Exeter: veiled city east of the lands of Dumnonia,
and here my mind always turns
to its red, pock-marked Devonian walls
and how the Cornish-speaking masses
were exiled beyond their boundary
and so trekked as stupified cattle to the west
to stay in a corner of the world assigned to them.
(For spite, they showed them later on
that they wouldn't be corralled
and so went out, sailed in ships
and dug holes in every land ever since,
deep enough to declare, 'Dun't try that on again!')
But this was an age of occupation,
when the Anglo-Saxons seemed to control all.
In so doing, we wrote our stories and they wrote theirs.
I have occupied my years studying both:
the turgidity (if we are honest) of *Ordinalia*'s doubting Thomas,
the misery and hope of Saint Meriasek,
the heavy chough-laden writings of Nance,
the voices who still carry their resistance.
Likewise too, I have turned pages of the Anglo-Saxon.
Here the *Codex Exoniensis*, the so-called 'Exeter Book'
– one end of a see-saw that has Causley and Dartmoor at its fulcrum.
This side, the bounce of 'The Seafarer' and its opening line:
'I can sing a true song of myself'.
That is a song I have always tried to follow.

Here too, the ninety-six riddles
that spin out of the manuscript
as bright as the conundrum of white swans
who now float and gleam upon the River Exe.
These games – both religious and secular
must have delighted the occupiers
who sat in streets where once gabbled the Troyance tongue.
So just as we named our world in Ælfric's vocabulary –
from God Almighty downwards to the lowly horse saddle,
so they riddled what mattered

into puzzles of bulls, bellows, book-moths
and the *double-entendre* of the humble onion:
'*Staþol min is steapheah stonde ic on bedde neoðan ruh nathwær*'
[My stem is erect. I stand up in bed, hairy somewhere down below].
You hear Leofric's laughter at the ribald innuendo:
this great work of the tenth-century Benedictine revival.
The entanglement of the codex lives with me daily,
Gordian knots tossed across the centuries,
back and forth between this Exeter and me.

Today, on the cathedral green
and a new kind of riddling pun,
a language that is hard to understand,
worse than the mutations or englynnion of Middle Cornish,
kennings or scydlings in Anglo-Saxon.
Here a swathe of make-shift tents muddy
the tranquility of the Church of Saint Peter.
Shelters, slogans and sleeping bags
make for a gaudy village of protest.
Pizza packaging is improvised into posters,
while media snap this outlandish anarchy.
This is another occupation,
their wish for power relations to be fairer,
to de-stabilize global finance systems,
that benefit the few and not the many.
'We are the 99%' and 'Global Democracy NOW!'
New riddles here then, that only
Facebook and Twitter can solve.
So now inequality is challenged
beneath the sandstone façade of the Resurrection.
Inside, centuries-stable misericords are unseated,
the famous astronomical clock stops.
Above, the vaulting shudders; ceiling bosses fracture.
The bishop clasps his hands in frustration,
all 'People must exercise their right to protest peacefully'
but underneath afraid of what might truly transpire,
what might occupy minds instead of Bible and BSkyB.

It is the Christian Athelstan who occupied this place too.
Took what he wanted from my people.
and expelled protest, all democracy, called them 'filthy'
because they spoke in riddles he couldn't break.
A missal records how he sent out for (like Domino's pizza)
'a little piece of the bush in which the Lord spoke to Moses',
'the candle which the angel of the Lord lit in Christ's tomb',
all to help him justify his imperialism.
Soon then, authorities will, like this King,
be occupied with expulsion, here in Exeter and elsewhere too,
and new turf can be laid upon the pristine green as if nothing had
    happened.
The message is no riddle,
no Anglo-Saxon nor Brythonic rhyme
Christ always occupied what he disliked
but with modern Athelstans about,
no-one seems to say this anymore.
Too much holy twig, too much holy candle-light.

Riddle solved then.
Don't upset the apple-cart.
Don't rock the boat.
Don't speak that tongue.
Stay where you are meant.
Stick to your usual occupations.

Yet as enigma, as puzzle, as rebus,
still, 'I can sing a true song of myself'.

Illuminations

You come for opposites:
      East, instead of West,
North, instead of South.
You come for the Anglo-Saxon,
instead of the Brythonic.
You come for illuminated gospels
instead of your *Pascon Agan Arluth*.
You come, because you want to know
the ideology and inner core
of your oppressor.
You want light shone.
Don't you?

You know the sick truth of our islands
      but still you come to *this* island.
Your people probably called it Medcaut.
Everyone else names it Lindisfarne.
It is Holy Island, famed for its healing.

First, comes the bleak causeway.
      Leave the Great North Road
and follow the tide table.
Keep to the designated path.
Check the raised shelters by the side of track.
You become the fog, as you try to see.

Park now in demarked car parks –
      room enough for a thousand vehicles.
Catch a bus down to the castle.
The stump of it magically struts
over the flatness.
You recall its use in Polanski's *Macbeth*.
You see the light of the world behind it.
You know how those monks were inspire

Take the climb towards it
        and note the seabirds' feet
that gloop in the harbour ink.
Behind the castle
see the overturned herring fleet hulks
made into storage sheds.

Back in the village
        the past is gilded.
St Alban and Bede
step forward.
Gospels are illuminated
in cabinet and display.

This is 'English Heritage'
        – a force I know well –
who show a story
of invasion upon invasion
in apostolic succession:
Celt loses to Anglo-Saxon
who loses to Viking
who loses to Norman
who all lose to
*The Ecclesiastical History of
the English People.*

Never mind though.
        I can buy coasters
with Cotton. MS Nero DIV on them,
or purchase Folio 27
wrapped around a chocolate bar.
This power dislocates.
Prompts disquiet
in this most quiet of places.

Bede is full of men
           whose name began with *Athel*,
and who you know were opposites
to those who called this place Medcaut.
You know those battles,
those exchanges, fusions,
those impregnations,
those subtle generational changes,
that historians speak of and give light to.

By the time you have emerged
           from the heritage centre,
the fog has cleared.
It is light.
Levered in, is the Priory itself,
a confusion of buildings and periods.
You pay to see ruination,
and wonder at those
who worked the scriptorium,
and noted, very occasionally the fate
of those in opposing climes to them:
Dumnonia, Hehil and Hingeston Down,

Now, history does not matter.
           In the village shops
Celt and Anglo-Saxon are blended,
like the coffee at Pilgrims cafe.
They are sold the same
as we are on the same path, aren't we?
Anyway, all interlocked knotwork
looks the same.
Throw Viking in there too
and all is complete.
Dissenters cannot compete
with the way History is spun.

The tide is turning and I must go.
        I've had healing on Holy Island
because this land of sand and mudflat
is microcosm of a wider island's fate.
Sometimes in opposites,
we see ourselves.
The word is truer there somehow,
the gospel keener,
the light brighter.

III

Conversations with a Breton Woodsman

Sawdust sticks to the sweat on his philtrum,
this moist August, here in *Melioneg*,
where his bark-born hands guide timber
from the woods at *Ar Gemene* and *Lanwelan*.

Eighty years old this summer, he tells me,
through his rattling wooden teeth.
Such dentures fit this man of trees:
his gob filled with what he knows best.

He thinks me mad, crazy even.
I am conversing in the dust of Cornish,
hoping some splinters will pierce,
and make it through the grind of separation.

In the woodshed, his work and life mingle.
He shows me Breton books and journals,
mangled by damp, frost and time.
Their fonts are coated with shavings.

The spinning blade splinters a log.
Its metal teeth chomp through rings of time
and the trunk is eased through by him.
Outside, as debris, lie all those branches.

The brutal cut of history severs us
into two emergent planks:
one knotted and gnarled; the other straight and firm.
You know which one he keeps.

His apron is sap soaked; his cap an acorn.
"Do you speak Breton every day?" I ask.
"Yes. Every day – I know no French.
And you – with Cornish?"

"Occasionally," I try to say.
His puzzled face becomes a canopy of leaves.
My land is still a sapling.
His, a forest.

Les alignements de Carnac

In seeing them   the first temptation is to align   everything.

It is a search for order.   control,   obsession,

so phones, cutlery,   cheese   are pressed into rows.

I make miniature Carnacs: runs of rock   on beaches or bark.

Even quoits of bread, fruit passage tombs,   marker stones of Euros.

Everything is pressed to stand,   to point,   to sit.

No entropy here.   Each must erect   the earth.

I know my task.   I am builder, seer,   stander.

They will stay put,   poke   and mystify.

The compulsion is   endless,   nameless

yet in me,   and my being   and heart.

Odd. for the poet this   I always thought   his mission

was to be outside   looking in.

the row

So I scatter, create chaos, bring disorder, bastardy, naughtiness.

Alignments topple,
    fall and snap.
        like the huge stone at Locmariaquer.
        It is a fallen Diplodocus.

I know my calling. I know my stone. It is the stone of the poet.

I am
the
lone
menhir.
and
I will
watch
time
grow.

Calais Migrants' Church

As if a station,
from a Medieval Passion,
it rises.

Lengths of wood and patches of canvas
tied with string and leather;
the detail worked by cable ties.

Above sits a rough-hewn crucifix,
carried from somewhere distant
by someone here.

Crates form an altar,
and Bibles in many tongues
coalesce and merge.

It has come together from nothing,
just as its congregation
has done.

Each day this community prays.
Each night this community
dances with Eurostar,

cuts fences, lifts razor wire,
plays cat-and-mouse with security,
all in the name of a better life.

For some though,
this church is their only hope.
They sing, pray, commune

yet new realms.
and their Jerusalem
are just as far away as ever.

Pont des Arts, Paris

Steel jowds,
brass clooties.
decorate the span
across the Seine.

Their metal shimmers
in the Spring light
where lovers make a tryst:
clasp, sealed by clasp.

Scratch your names
on the fob.
Find a release of wire
and snap it shut.

There.

Throw the keys into the deep
so they may never be found.
Love is then sealed,
preserved forever.

The Bridge of Love
bends and creaks at this art.
Migrant lock-sellers
run from *gendarmarie*.

Now, each time we doubt,
my mind travels to that lock.
It is tougher than both of us.
and binds me to you,

Though brass and steel
may one day rust,
it won't be before our dust
is carried by the Seine to the sea.

Model Sailboats,
Jardin du Luxembourg, Paris

So simple this –
wood, sail and stick
are age old.
All they need is wind and luck.
They have transversed this ornate basin
for generations:
all those watching seeking delight
in their crossings and circumlocutions.
Paris light silhouettes their flight,
their desire for Godspeed.

Around this watery globe
spin tackers on trikes
who poke, push and shove
yachts on journeys of fate.
They smile and wonder
as each boat reaches distant shores
while the Eiffel sail looks on

There we are, as adults –
boat-bulders, cap'ns, crew
patiently waiting for the same,
wondering, waiting
for each voyage.

We all drift by,
on our fervent navigations
broken destinations
and still, the children smile
and hope.

Meditation at the Grave of Jim Morrison in Père Lachaise Cemetery, Paris, August 2014

Avenues of Death,
and mausoleums where
one-upmanship
means that the Gothic layers Gothic.
Most dwellings are garden sheds of Funarae;
shelters where prayers are offered.

On the hillside,
the palaces of passing grew:
Neo-Classical homage
to lives now utterly forgotten.
All are displays of power
where tombs echo Parisian mansions
and decoration shows place and position.

All are packed in,
nice and cozy for the afterlife.
All neighbours in Elysium.
You wonder at the decay,
the lack of maintenance,
but then see the hidden glory.

Stone, once white as snow,
is now blackened
from a thousand Parisian fires.
Soot and grime sit solemn.

The newly dead are still
being tipped in.
There are blank headstones
for those next in line,
to those who will
leave town house and balcony
and come to live here,

Their carved names at least will last,
even if the memory fades.

In the cobbled streets where once mourners stood
now tourists plot their way through tombs:
Selfies by Oscar Wilde
Snapshots by Chopin,
Posts of Edith Piaf.
Iron has now rusted on all of them,
and grills split and decay.
Mass nettles weave their way through headstones.

Somewhere in this confusion of death, I find
Morrison.
I stand before you Jim.
You, now enclosed in stone.
Your grave daubed with messages.
covered in photos,
a barrier in place to stop those
wild enough to make love on top of you.
But then you always knew of sex and death,
death and sex.

You're a long way from California.
Long Beach is a way away.
'Strange Days', indeed.

Votive candles burn –
as many as found inside Notre Dame.
There are messages.
You, like all the others:
Keats, Chatterton, Hendrix, Cobain,
knew you place.

Your resting place is tiny,
tucked in behind others
of more status.

This is where the fashionable dead
of Paris head.

Decadence and decline
crawl up between
the slabs and kerbstones.
But you knew this Jim.
You knew it all along.
They grasp at their own skeletal effects,
their own hopes and highs.

Mindful of Revolution,
1789 to 1969
– when the tourists go –
those like Jim here,
light fires, ride storms.

Meanwhile, the dead,
in ivied tomb and catacomb,
try to break on through
to the other side.

Ca' Rezzonico

Venice knows

how to be a nation,

or at least, knows what it could be.
There is no pause, no intermission.

It speaks through

all tongues and times.

History oozes here,

is steamed out of the Lattes in St Mark's Square,

from distant lake dwellers,
to those who baked the first clay bricks,

and built upwards

through the rushes and fish.

From the moment

you step out

from Santa Lucia railway station,
life, language, identity – are all here.

It is a nation

that smacks the senses.

Ludicrously,

it has rivers as streets.

Everywhere run shafts and adits of blue,
which are trammeled and tributed

    by rich and poor,

        the old and young.

There is, in everything,

    a decayed elegance,

of knowing that which was once powerful – is no more.
This is a trinket of truth I take back

    to my land

        and its posturing.

The unpretentious nation

    breathes with boats.

They are its oxygen, its very lungs.
I take a sweaty vaporetto

        down the length

           of the Grand Canal.

And watch

    this nation be washed away,

though all have the resolve,
to stop the dissipation,

                    the subtle erosion
                            of its imagined self.

Inside

            the packed waterbus

I note others have come for this,
to see resistance and refuge,

            to look beneath

                    bridge and canal.

I get out

            at Ca' Rezzonico

and its towering marble façade.
Here the baroque dominates

            as most tourists

                    pause for selfies.

Instead, alone,

                    I climb to the mezzanine floor

knowing already the pattern,
and that this was Browning's nation;

            home of so many

                    meditations.

As I wander,
            I recall all those lines

from 'My Last Duchess', 'Fra Lippo Lippi'
and 'A Grammarian's Funeral'

            drilled into me

                        when still young and keen.

The ghost of you

            is here too Jack

shuffling through these rooms
with Ruth holding your hand.

            It's all a long way, boy.

                                    from Goonamarris Slip.

For me too,

            this is unworldly,

an inversion of state and being
unknown democracy,

            unfathomable,

                        as alien as life on Earth gets.

Outside soon snaps back,

                        and the full nation strives again,

mining water, quarrying silt
with barges carrying clay away.
    Clay and water, nation and self –

        endless cycles, that still cause my work to flow.

IV

Letters from the Land of the Long White Cloud

for Allen Curnow (1911-2001)

He wahine, he whenua, e ngaro ai te tangata.
[By women and land are men lost]
                                        Māori Proverb

I   Maraetai Shells

In my mind you are picking up shells
on the beach at Maraetai,

looking out over Tamaki Strait,
on, on towards the Coromandel.

There you will find scallops,
oysters and conch shells.

I like the way your hair
falls down the back of your neck.

It makes a line
as hard as greenstone.

The cloud is white and long today.
A land of it - as the Māori say.

In my mind,
this is the way it is.

But the shells still swash
and no shadow falls on Tanaki.

Instead, gently,
it crosses my heart.

II By Mount Taranaki

Your skin

    is as white
        as the snow on Mount Taranaki.

As perfect too.

    It binds with the earth,
        the way sea and sky here do.

That is old.

    Newer still
        are the streets of New Plymouth

    where wonders and wanderers

    built new lives,
        made new loves.

Miles away,

    I feel your ice turn to water,
        sense you melt inside.

III   Saturday Night in Hokitika

Saturday Night in Hokitika,
and the great Tasman Sea
is blowing in hard.
Winds that touched Africa days ago
now hit here.

In summer they flock
for the beach and surf,
but tonight
it is mid-August,
and a winter night.

Youths in hoodies
walk Sewall Street
and Weld Lane,
knowing not what to do
or where to go.

The headline of the local paper
– the *West Coast Mercury* –
celebrates the re-opening
of a toy library.
I feel them sigh, feel their anger.

The sea mist consumes all,
hiding Māori gift shops,
jade stone, cafés,
ambition, drive, escape.
All is familiar.

For kicks, an old cinema –
colonial-style - still opens.
A sign there still advertises
'talking movies'.
Tonight, it is *Harry Potter*.

So at least,
for two hours,
the young of Hokitika
might fantasise, pretend,
and live anywhere but here.

The knowing of this
forces a tear.
My familiar Hokitikas
call me loudly,
back across the seven seas.

IV   Pebble towers at Bruce Bay, Highway 6

For
a break
on the long road to Haast,
pull over at Bruce Bay.

There,
each passer-by
has added to pebble art,
and white towers rise on the beach.

Each
pebble is its own spirit level,
an intricate weaving of balance and air.
This is nature's jenga.

The
tide judders your tower.
This far down,
lines of longitude touch Antarctica.

Hold
your nerve,

while rock meets rock.
Ease a tor into shape.

Their
line stretches to the horizon
where sea spray catches the light
for a Tate-style installation.

The
final pebble I'm readying to place
I forego and pocket.
Over-ambition's never good.

Instead,
its mass will travel with me
across tropic and equator
coming to rest in the
logan of your

hand.

V   Cornish Miner's Cottage, Arrowtown

1.   Lay un out straight,
     an' make sure ee d'face south.

2.   Be close t'the Bank
     so you'n save a bit.

3.   Have a shed out back
     fur winter wood.

4.   Make sure tha' chapel
     ent too far mind.

5.   Be minded of the way feythur
     built ut back St Just.

6. Buy saffron, read the Bible.
    Befriend the Chinks. Fuck the Irish.

7. Be far enough away from
    the rough buggers from Thames.

8. Never leave your shovel an' gads outside.
    They'll 'ave um soon as look at ee.

9. Be minded of how far
    you are from home.

10. Put kiddle on. Make taa.
    Count blessin's.

VI   Cornishman's Dam, Gabriel's Gully, Otago

Did you
pig-headed
coozened Jacks
get any further than this?

Probably not,
until you
take on stoping
on the Planet Mars,

or the price
of tin goes
exponential
on the Dow Jones Index.

For now,
your dam
for sluicing
is left in unforgiving forest,

where winter
frost coats
silver ferns
and marshy tussocks prevent me

from seeing
your ghosts –
you Varcoe,
you Hancock and you, boy Hore.

Of course,
you needed water
at the valley head
to wash, sieve and shake your lives,

iron guttering
and pipes
tumbling down
to your tramming and buddles,

all gone now,
this bright
August day,
turned into picnic spots and trampers' walks.

At least
I find your
slatted wood chapel,
high on the dusty Blue Spur Road

above the
dig-holes
of the Gully
where once the whole world swarmed.

Wrecked
long-toms

and winzes
are still there though, as anachronisms,

the native forest
destroyed
like a tornado
went through only yesterday.

Your dam
still
holds me though -
a pool of dark thought

across
the gullies
of time –
a blood launder running deep into the soul.

Hard to
mind ut
now boy.
It always comes to the surface.

The poet's job
is to open
flood gates,
break levees, pan for gold.

VII Moeraki Boulders

They are spheres
as if dropped by the gods by accident.

I have my own narratives
– how stones become so.
Pixies usually the guilty party.

The Māori say they are baskets,
left by early expeditionary canoes,
and turned by magic into rock.

These globes scatter the beach here,
perfect worlds set in sand.
The sun is setting
and their density merits
all the vastness the Pacific can muster.

On a single globe,
I mark my position,
noting a satisfaction
with this, with all, with nothing.

Turning to another spot
upon this boulder
I note imperfections
this August evening.

Here, in this land of Aotearoa
Adidas is being critiqued
for the mark up on All Blacks' jerseys,
while in London Adidas-clad rioters
walk on streets I know well.
These are the worlds
of Hackney, of Tottenham –
so foreign now.

The peace here is not known to everyone,
but magic can't always make perfection.

And tonight, Moeraki's flaws
        help me
                to leave the pixies behind.

VIII   Imagined Edoras

Back here at Edoras,
        where in Tolkien's mind,
King Théoden ruled.

Jackson gave it a reality,
        on the hillock
below Mount Potts' Station.

These are the horse lands,
        knot-work adorning shield and spear,
now imagined at the world's end.

J.R.R. walked Cornwall's cliffs,
        and found Stokes' Meriadoc.
Good enough for Merry Brandybuck.

It is just as I imagined it,
        growing up beneath Hensbarrow,
and reading the trilogy to escape.

Now it is I who have left,
        to travel my own Middle Earth,
a lone *Origo Mundi* in Rohan,

Goodbye then, to the bastarding clay,
        and the Cornish capacity
for intolerance, inferiority, inaction.

You are back there now,
        maybe waiting for a ring,
and I am here, on these vast plains.

Today, you will be Éowyn
        and I shall be Aragorn.
Together, we shall each disappoint.

IX   Engine House, Kawau Island

At home, you're two a penny.
    so many that we become oblivious
and not notice any more.
        You're seen the postcards though:
of Wheal Coates reaching down
into heather cliffs, into azure sea,
You know Crowns Mine,
    nestled into Botallack's crunch.
There, the stones are said to swirl overhead
    in the levels under the ocean.

An ocean or two away, near Kawau Island,
    even the pilot does not want to take me across.
It is their winter and the Jellicoe Channel's rough today.
    On the bumpy approach, are holes in the earth
where my people came to dig.
    There are adits running towards the cliffs,
probably once full of false promises,
    that or blistering finds of copper.

On top of Kawau is a graveyard,
    the wooden crosses all but gone,
but a laminated list records the names
    of all the Cousin Jacks who braved this hellhole.
Fittingly, they are now all covered in lush ferns.
    There is a soft end for calloused hands.

You're not ready for the sight at Miner's Point.
  The slippery clay takes you to an engine house.
The Pacific pitches in more showers
  and a mizzle, just like home, persists.
Mine and stack barely grip the sea-level rock.
  It seems as if at any time, the ocean might consume them.

I feel the worked stone, the fine brickwork,
  testament to those who took the ships
from Plymouth to New Plymouth
  and had to stank across a new world to be here.
In all this, I see my people's struggle,
  their quest in the earth,
endeavour, wonder and hope.
  At places like this, times like these,
with my pen, I swear to keep digging,
  to extrapolate, to mine, to recover
my nation's hewn and hammered history.

X   The Forest Seals at Ohau Point Stream

My tongue names them *royne*.
    The Māori call them *kekano*.
    You know them as *seals*.
Here, at rushing Ohau Point
    the pups ascend the fuming river valley
    and frolic uninhibited in a plunge pool.

The patient mothers bring them here in winter
    to this woodland kindergarten
    until they are ready for the ocean's pull and press.
They are ergonomic mermaids
    who twist and turn and chatter
    beneath the cool, cascading water.

Seals in a forest doesn't compute.
        They sit proud amongst leaf and lichen,
        instead of rough barnacle and rock.
The whole forest is charmed by them
        as if the sea runs the land
        and salt controls each branch and bud.

These beings have done so for a thousand years
        and, at this, bark, clap flippers, smile
        and know this is their realm.
As humans we can only marvel,
        and try hard not to be jealous
        at this, their devolved world.

I watch their unoppressed joy
        In the water, they make their rules.
        write their own law,
and we, we people of
        the cornered land-sea-land-sea
        must have another thousand years of patience.

XI   Kaitiakitanga*

My people have been bad.
They deserve to be punished.
Naughtiness runs in their Brythonic veins.

They have hacked, hewn,
carved and taken.
There are monuments to this everywhere –
in holes, pits and shafts.
Now we view them
with an amazed guilt.

How should we walk
on a land
criss-crossed with such a past?

Paths merge and converge,
fluid as high-speed rail-tracks,
lines of song across centuries.

A shame enters me each day,
a collective shame
at what we have become.
I see changes, I see disrespect.
I see a land too small:
a victim of its own success.

Implosion then, the only way.
Like the people of Rapa Nui
who, when they walked too heavily,
upon their isolation,
toppled their stone heads
for shame and pity.

It is hard; bitter even,
tasteless as sea-salt,
tough as granite
sticky as clay,
but each day I try to tread
a little lighter.

* From the Maori concept of guardianship of the land.

XII Renewal at Ahipara

At Ahipara
I can escape
the bonds my spiteful country has given me..

The shackles fall off.

The sands here are not
loaded with language anymore.
The sea's words
don't hold stories.
The land, for once, is not
prose, poem or play.

The horizon is just that.
Shells give no metaphors.
Rock provides no allegory.
Yucca exist.
Kumara grow.
Hoki swim.
Tui fly.
Mussels do what they do.

In my imageless-ness
only then can I find me again.

Close by,
a Māori poet
begins his slow toil.

V

Interim Nation

We have a border.
We have a language.
We have a name.
We have a flag.
We have a parliament.
We have an anthem.
We have a past.
We have all this,
yet we have no nation.

One day there will be permanence,
passion and proof.
Until then, I will be a result of this
interim nation.

They think I'm awkward,
belligerent,
that I'm just provocative.
They're dismissive.

So there we are:
caught between two worlds –
county and country.
These are the two words
that trip up the Media,
that doubters love,
that those who rage against me conflate.

Let them have their say.
It means nothing.
Is nothing.

Throw rocks.
Dismiss me.
But I won't go away.
Maybe now I am still part,
half, bit, improper, interim.

One day though,
I promise,
words will shift and move,
and make us whole again.

Carne, Looking West

Here, twisted strands of gorse
coat the timeless hump.

Each day, wind takes sap in new directions:
vortexes are formed over decades.

They choose here with good reason:
the highest point
– fitting for a chieftain's commemoration.

Around and about, leys storm off
to Nare Head, the curve of Porthscatho,
the looming gasp of the River Fal.

The path across the field is old,
even through the furrows
ploughed last week.
Steel scraped back a soil
that once was holy and sacrosanct.

I have walked this carne
so many times:
threaded my life here; plaited woe and joy.

I come back for grounding,
longing, home.
I find fidelity with the ages;
some myelination with time.

From this pimple, upon the earth
I watch another sun set in the west.

Below my feet
the dead knew it as something else.

*Howlsedhas** is what they utter.

Yes, the living whisper back.

* Cornish: The West

Heritage

Is that – like – Seltic?

No. Celtic, I argue.

So – you a real Selt?

Yes.

How many Selts are there now?

Several. A few of us.

When abroad,
I sometimes find it best
to deny the English gene
that lurks in me.

It came in
– in a moment of madness
obviously,
when some great, great, great fool
got un wrong and let the pure bloodline slip.

Deep in age,
I put this down to
when I write in this *Seltic* tongue
I am unable to handle its complexities.
All those damned changing first letters,
that lenition,
and vowel affection.

At least, I am honest
with my heritage.

At least then,
a mutated *Selt*.

Man-Engine

You've seen
the sepia photographs:
felt-hatters and
sticking tommies
extending feet onto
slippery platforms.
Every stroke raises
you twelve feet.
Alternate steps from
one rod to the other.

Muscles grip for dear life,
and crowst over shoulder.
You must time ut zactly
t'make the jump.
Else it's oblivion.
Makes ee wince
at every crack,
wondering if thaas
the weak point boy,
so you ride un, laughing.

These have been there,
time out of mind.
As you step inches
your lungs contract,
They dig like drill bits,
place charges in your sternum.
You are a worker ant
vertically aligned,
but all could so easily
drop into the abyss.

The fat arse
of your pard
is just above
on the next platform.
The trace smell of his
nervous fart as you ascend.
Ladders rise and fall
seemingly at whim.
Shafts are connected to these
ladders of testosterone.

But there's naw other choice.
naw other way.
Some rods you d'knaw.
They shake in their sockets
at every judder.
Others are hard as tin,
lasting as old man's workings.
They'm cheeky as Knockies,
bolder than maids
come Anniversary.

Down here wars come and go.
Weather hits the cliffs
but you knaw nawthun.
'Tis blacker than Montol,
wet as mackerel.
Boot-print on wood
that wuz how twuz.
You went down on un.

I see them all,
all they felt-hatters,
stomping time
desperate for the light
three-points always touchin'
to be certain of naw fall.
Daily, they make
their leap of faith.

Yet we are here now,
stepping up, and on,
out of darkness
and into light.
Despite this game
of snakes and ladders,
all its tut and tribute,
we are still bringing
our world to grass.

You gibm bell tink,
they tommy stickers
then you'n up on un again.

This century and man-engines
have rotted away.
They've tumbled into the earth,
levered themselves off,
diving into the gloom
as here at Tresavean.
I gape at a hole
foreboding as Hell itself,
into which nimble men
stepped a tin ballet.

Elocution Lesson

They are the posh girls from Menheniot and Liskeard
who ride the packed train back to Cornwall each day.

They nestle in close, between
Primark shoppers and bored commuters.

They eat cake, text and view Instagram.
slag off mates and ex-boyfriends.

They are those that deemed a Cornish education
below them; it being too cakey. and too maazed.

They are sent to Plymouth's Grammars
where soul. accent and identity will easily be erased.

They are our future lawyers, doctors and engineers.
They should not speak like turnip.

They watch the Cornish get on and off
already knowing, at 14, the failings of their people.

They huddle so to escape the scum of their 'county'.
They'd call it nothing else, but this interim assault.

They speak a Standard English, fresh as rose oil,
to show they've entered a higher class.

At Saltash, the train stops by a sign
that welcomes the English to Cornwall.

The Cornish get on, in turnip mode:
smelly, loud, but speaking perfectly correct.

One winces, as a boy makes room and accommodates:
"Dun't ee worry m'andsome! You'm aright."

I smile at this genuine elocution.
and ask Wudn' ut be lovely?

Suddenly, he is Professor Henry Higgins
and she Miss Eliza Dodlittle.

Too soon though, he is back to phone Minecraft
and she confidently strides off at St Germans.

He carries on speaking like turnip,
while with BMW, daddy collects this fair lady.

Border Crossing

For Raymond Williams (1921–1988)

It can be anywhere
    on a line, a boundary, or a map,
    the most momentary of transitions:
a move from one place to another,
    one state of mind to the next,
    but always, you are with me.

I have walked your Black Mountains,
    admired your understanding of the Celt
    – set adrift – in an English system.
I understood your problem
    with materialism and culture.
    It was my problem too.

Before, I had only read literature.
    After you, I understood it.
    Then, I assumed the big ideas
– awareness, culture, class, identity
    didn't belong to me.
    But you taught me a way.

You still weave through me:
    Y Fenni to Henrik Ibsen,
    The Country and the City,
Keywords and *Dombey and Son,*
    Englishness, Welshness,
    and what lay in between.

Daily, I cross from Saltash to Plymouth,
    and see *Ker-land, Eng-now,*
    a border country you would know,
and still, your books
    – tiny resources of hope –
    are tucked deep in my satchel.

Cornish Shovel

Upright, in the far grove of the outhouse,
it stands as a druid's staff,
all-knowing eye of Baal scratched upon ut.
It is for secret ceremony and rite.
Still some dry trade on ut from the last dig,
while money spiders makes runs on its leading edge.
A fine earth falls when you d'grab un and move into the light.
'Twas boughten once, es, over 'Griggs Hardware',
but now fits its owner as a hand in a glove.
His calluses match the wood perfectly,
born of decades of dig, skim and drag.
Comfortable as the smell of taa and saffron.
In its time, it've shifted slimes and spar, tailings and trade.

The shaft is longer than English spades;
the squat ones they sell now in 'B&Q' and 'Homebase'.
'Made fur piskies they be.'
You'n swing more with this.
Less hurt on the back see.
Tis all t'do with the leverage,
the precise bend of knees and back,
that despite the bleddy rheumatism this year
makes the load easy,
the toil clever.

They do swear by ut still over allotment.
The blade's the right angle for levering over
the winter weeds and daishels.
Stank un in, then pull ov un back.
It d'come away like a bewdie then.
All ready for the spring teddies and cabbages.

In the wet earth, the blade glistens like granite.
This is a Cornish shovel.
Reav was the old word, in the time before the confusion of the
tongues
when there was still tribute, tut and bal-maidens enough.

The slight rust on the edge makes naw difference.
But there will always be questions:
'What ee need that fur s'much?'
If you knaw this shovel, you knaw why.
You shout back across time:
'Ee've dun that fur ee naw ebm a?'
Shovel d'belong here see.

This is a tool of the tin stream and claywork.
The blade's design is older
than the mossy roundhouses at Carn Euny;
probably first hammered and bent
on an anvil the day the cussing Phoenicians pulled in,
and stopped fur bit crowst on the cold Cassiterides.
Somewhere, it put the shimmering tin on Solomon's Temple,
helped carve the Lamb and Flag blocks on Ictis,
and had a part in the tale of John of Chyanhor.

In the mouldering sheds and outhouses
of Hensbarrow, Carn Brea and Carnmenellis,
in the dank valleys of Fowey, Fal and Camel,
pretty many they stand stiff as pikes, proud as Angov,
an army against dirt, dust and muck;
a palisade against change, modernity,
and all that is shovelled upon we from the east.
You knaw that despite constant burial
we always dig our way out.

But this is the shovel that built our world in the west
It dug our foundations and trenches,
shaped ground-works, sewers, kennals,
the launders and the lodes,
mixed mortar and moved earth.
It is Truro Cathedral.
It is Tesco.
It is boulder and bedding plant.
It is school and hospital.

It is mine and moor.
It is Celtic cross and VW camper car park.

And in its crescent of hard iron,
its gnarled staff, its pivot and pare
we come to know ourselves,
understand what must be lifted, turned and placed
for we resilient shovellers of the west.

Ode on the Mylor Hoard

Ground over,
now the artefact becomes the art. Fact.

Museum-held,
the find sits on blue velvet.
Now free, the thirty-three socketed axes
fan out like the rising sun's dawn rays
ceruse and copper-blue of hue,
soft as the clay water of distant Hensbarrow's quarries.
Their fiery edges point to a radiant orb
that is a caudled ceramic pot,
now cracked like desert river-beds
into volatile hexagons of time.

The open handle ends chant and sing.
Or perhaps stare as peering eye sockets,
and gaze into a skull past
away t'go there, t'Mylor
- probably from the Breton Meloir,
ancient abbot-bishop
but still a thousand dark years
after these spindly alloy heads
were secretly, lovingly hoarded
and placed into the earth's peaty care.

These are new castings though,
not worn or trusted blades
which chipped at tin, wood or bone.
Handles were never fastened.
No leather bindings were tied.
He dug this pit out purposefully,
overlooking the still creek of heron and crab,
carefully loading the vessel with fresh bracken
like it had meaning, like it mattered;
we know not to what purpose.

In too, stumbled blind caterpillars
who never became flickering butterflies,
insects, grasses, seeds and twigs,
items named differently then.
An earthen plug locked in the long centuries.
The axe heads never knew the mystery
that when Meloir was a child
his hands and feet were chopped off,
and replaced by heavy silver ones
which magically grew with him.

It is the magic of metal detection
which located this treasure,
a physic found where the field slopes due north.
Maybe it was once a frosty glade where
the Cordwainer players rehearsed
their Mummer's Christmas play,
not knowing what lay just beneath.
Here, in 1759 stanked Penty Ladin,
Bill Solomon and 'In-comes I' Johnny Rowe.
So spoke, wise as Meloir, their Turkish Knight:

"What place is are
What seens appare
Whare ever itorn mine eye
tis all around
in chantin ground.

Ground over,
now the artefact becomes the art. Fact.

Museum-held,
the find sits on blue velvet.

And now free, the thirty-three socketed axes
chant their fiery mysteries back to me.

Radicalised

I have become radicalised.

Yeah, me.
A white guy, who shouldn't have issues.

It happened when I first read Berresford Ellis.
He taught me another way.

It happened when I saw Cardiff spelt *Caerdydd*.
That taught me a new space and place.

It happened when I realised my difference.
That taught me the lies I been educated with.

It happened when I saw granfer again.
He taught me the ancient words handed down.

I won't be planting no bombs though.
I'll just write an explosion of words.
Take off a rucksack filled with history
and unpack a desire for change.

Is that enough?
Is that enough for you to raid me?
Is that enough for you to pin me down in the street?

So come on, water-board me.
Wrap the agony of towels and begin the drowning.
Torture me until I talk.

Play me the music that will 'fuck my God'.
Play it loud so I won't take it any more.
Torture me so I will talk.

So yeah, I'm radicalised.

See that MI5.

Know that Devon and Cornwall Constabulary.
Understand that *Tesco, McDonalds, Microsoft*
and all you other multinationals.

See this pen?

The terror makes it write.

Goodbye An Gof

Goodbye Michael Joseph.
Goodbye An Gof, boy blacksmith,
forger, hammerer, leader.
I am leaving you now
because I must.

I begin by saying goodbye to you
where I began – at St Austell.
Platform 2 – the line up-country.
It is a journey across a Britain
you knew well Michael.

This was always where my adventures began.
As boy here, I recorded numbers
in an Ian Allen locomotive book,
and snuck in the parcel room for warmth,
where uncle Treva Pasca ran affairs.
Sixteen saw me cross the footbridge
with a girl who taught me love.
We kissed and watched clay trains
rocket past to Burngullow Junction.
Then, it was a life packed up,
encased for university,
a suitcase of Rowse and Clemo.
Then latter days – trips east and west
have all begun here,
to Poland, New Zealand, USA,
but all have taken me back here
to rotting GWR wood
a platform where I know each dent
and can view the up-line.

Up there is intent, diffidence,
taxation, aggression,
a view of us.

Away then,
away from the same noose
you endured,
Away then,
away from the pity and hope,
away from dream and failure.
Cheers an' gone Michael.
Benetugana Angov.
Comero weeth.

Today, and another journey ahead of me.
away from turbulence,
the same maelstrom you knew.
The pink and blue HST
is forty years old.
Each time I travel I can't help but notice
'British Rail' still etched
in its door windows;
a scrawl even Thatcher could not erase.

You knew that Britain Michael.
You knew its wars, its island,
its fight; its oppression.

The train is full of gadgets
to which people must connect.
Everywhere is a profusion of
laptops, tablets and phones.
They feed the same lies you knew Michael.

Yet, still so different now.
I resist like we've always done
and think of Britain and us,
us and Britain.
Miles away, Scotland
is having a referendum
yet we still stick into the sea

We are still a GWR holiday poster.
We are still Duchy, Riviera, and Padstein.

The train trundles
across landscapes of resistance:
The palace at Lostwithiel,
Bodmin, home of your friend Flamank,
the Priory at St Germans,
where my predecessor,
John of Cornwall wrote his world,
then to Athelstan's marker,
the shitty brown of the Tamar
water that once preserved us
and kept us in aspic.

No-one else thinks of this,
this still morning.
as we clank and rattle
over the Royal Albert Bridge.
But I am trying to say goodbye.

These thoughts haunt me,
bully me, play on me.
They pull me back.
My father in '76 on a day trip to Bath.
Treva Pasca blawin' the whistle,
Bernard Bunt picking up the morning papers,
that pre-tablet, pre-Google, pre-Kindle
brought the world to me.
These were men with traces of you Michael,
genes of your resistance,
of your refusal.

In me too.

See, these are the memories
that have formed me.

I have been moulded by their take
on how 'tis, how it should be
and wasson next.
They are, I have discovered,
inescapable.

I have tried from London,
to the limits of where I have travelled,
as far as I could go,
to forget,
yet the further away
the more they track back,
pulling me,
connecting me like inverted parabola.

I do not want to go back,
but I must.
It does not matter
how often I try say
Goodbye An Gof,
– I have had enough –
that will, that frenzy, the anvil
that stoic sense of self,
always hammers its way back.

Legacy

poems are confetti

tossed over the heads

of brides and grooms

who never want to know them

and brush them off their shoulders

they over-reach

strive

aim as high

as Wordsworth, Keats, and Shelley

or Harris, Hawker, and Quiller Couch.

most weather away

merge into the soil

or become the food of slugs

their colours run to mud

their shapes spoil in the wet

it has always been the same

where are those not in any canon?

any nation's literature?

any people's past?

despite all though

some of the union remains

in damp churchyards

among grave and bramble

the legacy

of this marriage of words

quietly persists.

Rusty Country

for Philip Payton

Sometimes,
               when I look to my damp country

it seems crammed with rust: .

$2Fe(s) + 2H_2O(l) + O_2(g) \longrightarrow 2Fe^{2+}(aq) + 4OH^-(aq)$ everywhere,

and broken
          pieces of our past
                    are shattered,
         and reticent;
their oxidisation a boundary,
         a wire fence around them.

Today is another General Election,
         and more pieces of our rusty past
              are pretended to be swept away,
            to make way for new.
We will be cleaned up, and all this tat somehow wiped off
the busy earth we were always a part of.

There is buddle and bob,
durn and dry,
plunger and pump,
that flake an iron skin
as if they are bright orange reptiles
basking in yards and brown-field sites.

The jaws of kibbles, corrode into nothingness
at their last scoop of glory,
falling into mossy water.
Meanwhile, the wheels of skips cease to turn.

Drills lock, and winzes freeze.
WD40 too weak for they now.

It you've ever walked beyond
what we are marketed as
- what politicians want us to be -
and found a truth
in bracken, fern and bramble,
then you know of what I talk.

Know all those musty sheds
of the men of Cornwall,
who've saved in webbed jam-jars and Furniss biscuit tins,
the rusting screws and nails of tomorrow.
They are stowed there for the revolution
Homers, saved up for when the country's ready.
They are kept in case,
we should rise up, phoenix-like,
and reclaim our part, our iron, our metal.

It is in the places that built us,
that have had their ferrous hearts away,
Botallack and Geevor,
Crofty and King Edward,
Drinnick and Goonvean,
the hulks of the Fal,
the rusting rivets of the Royal Albert Bridge.

This was never enough though.
Rust is there too, in the dusty booklets
of the Cornish Language Board,
where staples leak a brown oxidisation,
as if being a lesser used language was not enough,
and the wiry speakers of this rusty tongue
wanted another way
to say we're here:
brittle, neglected, but still alive.
So, rust in the language then –
and rust in the levels and lodes;
rust in our verbs and past participles,

rust in the shafts and shaking tables.

Was it always the way?

It is as if we let it in,
welcomed it,
and accepted it as the way it should be.

We are out of practice,
naive.
permeable.

How did this happen?

Still in us though,
still deep,
is that structural integrity.

Now galvanise it.
Shine again.